Who put a Lizard in my Lasagna?

Using the Best
of Who You Are
to Create the Bes[t]
of What You Wan[t]

by Sam Glenn
"The Authority on Attitude" ™

Published By Everything Attitude, Inc.
608 S, Washington, Ste 207 • Naperville, IL 60540 • 800-818-6378
EverythingAttitude.com • Samglenn.com • Lizardbook.com

Chapters

"The greatest good you can do for another is not just to share your riches, but to reveal to him his own."

Benjamin Disraeli

 # It's not what you have - but how you use what you have - which determines your success.

Years ago while working out at the gym, next to me running on the treadmill happened to be Shaq (Shaquille O'Neal - professional basketball player). For those who don't know, he is a rather tall, large and successful basketball player, towering at 7 feet 2 inches. Even though, I am 6'7, I resembled the likeness of a pimple next to him.

Shaq is also somewhat of an attraction. As we worked out, people walked by and were star gazed by his presence. They stared at him with a sparkle in their eyes – like they were in the presence of greatness. At that moment, I caught a glimpse of my purpose. I thought, what if I could get people to look at themselves the same way, to see the treasure chest of greatness in themselves? Imagine opening a treasure chest to find valuable items – imagine the look on your face, the blood flow, the rapid beating of your heart. You might even scream with excitement. I know I would! Imagine looking in the mirror and know that greatness is staring you back.

I have got news; you do have that treasure chest of greatness inside of you. Many miss it because they are so hung up trying to be something they are not, comparing themselves to others, making excuses, doing things that lack substance, and doubting the abilities and gifts they were born with.

This book is about accessing the treasure chest of your potential, and discovering the gifts, abilities and resources, ready to be used to help you get where you want to be and achieve what you desire.

I embrace the story told by the late Earl Nightingale, Acres of Diamonds, about a farmer who sold everything to join a diamond rush. He wanted to be rich, so he sold his farm and set out to find wealth in the form of diamonds. Years went by with little luck. He exhausted his finances and finally gave up and died because he had no success. On the back end, the person who purchased his farm was walking along the property one day and discovered shiny stones in the creek on the farm property. It turns out the creek was full of diamonds. The farmer set out to find his fortune, when the fortune was already with him. Our treasure is already with us as well. And I plan to prove that to you in the following pages.

What do you want that will bring your life more meaning, happiness and fulfillment?

The foundation of my message began years ago sitting front row listening to Mark Victor Hanson, coauthor of the best-selling book series, <u>Chicken Soup for the Soul</u>, say these words, *"Whatever you want in life, know this... it wants you more."*

I thought, *"What a profound statement!"* I went home and really explored what he said. I wanted – or should I say, had a need for – a lot of things. I needed a bed to sleep in, a car that could go from A to B and then hopefully back to A (without the added assistance of a tow truck), and finally enough money to eat and pay bills. It doesn't seem like much, but as simple to attain as those things may seem, they were things I lacked at the time. I had a limited vision and outlook on my life.

My list of needs and wants has changed considerably since then, but the question that kept popping up into my mind over and over again was, *"How do I actually <u>get</u> to what I want; or if <u>it</u> really wants me more, how does <u>it</u> get to me?"*

In asking such a question, I felt like one of my college professors from philosophy class who only asked one question for the full semester, "What is piety?" I still don't know, and honestly don't care. The only question I wanted to answer was, *"How do I actually get to what I want; or if it really wants me more, how does it get to me?"*

I set out on a journey to find the answer. I got proactive and attended goal-setting workshops, kept a journal, pasted pictures of things I needed and wanted on the wall. I thought about what I wanted over and over again. I did whatever others did and told me to do, thinking it would ultimately be enough to answer the question, **how do I get more of what I want, or how does it get to me?**

And while all of those actions are **very** helpful and have been proven to assist in reaching success for many, there is actually another important step –a step so small, yet so significant to the cause of getting what we want– it can oftentimes be overlooked. I actually stumbled upon it and that's how I found it. And for that, I am grateful and excited to share the experience with you.

I want to unveil something special to you through the following pages, something that will truly make a difference and help you achieve whatever you want wherever you are. I am not talking about revealing a secret, or unlocking the hidden keys to this or that, or discovering 13 essential elements to something. *My focus is on a tool that will show you how to use the best of who you are to create the best of what you want.* The concept of this book is so simple that perhaps some might not grasp it, which I hope is not the case. We happen to live in times where it has become too easy to complicate simplicity.

It's very important to recognize that this book is about much more than acquiring "stuff." Things come and go; that's their nature. Although some stuff is rather nice to have, I want to take you to a dimension of life that goes *beyond* "stuff." I mean, who really needs another reason to have a garage sale? After a bit, a collection of stuff can do that. Some people pursue and hold onto material items as if they mean everything. As if they have the power to grant fulfillment.

For instance, there once was a man who hoarded his money like it was everything. Nothing wrong with saving, but he was obsessed and selfish with his money. When people would say, *"You know, you can't take your money with you!"* he would defiantly tell them, *"You just watch; I'm taking my money with me when I die!"* He stashed it away in a trunk in the attic and would not spend, share, or donate it. All he wanted to do was acquire it. He never took his wife out, never helped his children or others, never even indulged in a Sunday night ice cream cone. What is sad is that his money lacked vision or purpose, and as a result, his relationships grew empty and his everlasting legacy meaningless. Of course, inevitably the day came when he passed away. After the funeral, someone asked, *"So do you think he took his money with him?"*

They went up to the attic to check. When they opened the trunk, the money was still there. Someone in the room said, *"Well, I guess he didn't take it with him after all!"* Sarcastically, his wife said, *"If he wanted to take it with him, he should have buried it in the basement."*

Ouch! What a sad example of wasted resources and a misplaced importance on material things! Sadly, he hadn't just misused his money, but he had also wasted his heart. He failed to give of himself, and as a result, he left the world with no lasting legacy of kindness, love, charity, or generosity. His family only remembered how tightly he clung to his money. It would appear that in the end, though he had an attic-full of money, he had failed to achieve true fulfillment, peace or happiness. Had he really believed he was fulfilling his needs with that trunk full of money?

The truth is that what we really desire deep down at our core is happiness, security, comfort, fulfillment, peace and satisfaction. Think about it for just a moment: whatever it is you most desire, deep down you want the feeling you'll get from having it even more. Ultimately, we all want to feel fulfilled.

The BIGGER picture is that we can use the best of who we are to create something meaningful that will outlive our time on earth in a positive way. This is creating a **legacy**. What will people remember of you when your time on earth is done? What will you leave behind? I recently did some research on the late James C. Penney (of the JC Penney department stores). Take some time to research his story. It's quite extraordinary. He was passionate about serving people, giving much of his time and finances to philanthropic causes throughout his life. He was able to create a lasting legacy by using the best of who he was *(his unstoppable vision and passion)* to create the best of what he wanted *(wealth, fulfillment, contributions, opportunities, employment, etc.)*.

What you are about to read is an account of an experience that began a little more than a decade ago. The lesson began in my very small apartment. The entire experience changed my life - but more importantly, opened my eyes - to my ability to build something that will last far beyond my time here on earth. This concept is so exceptional to the cause of achievement, I have used it to generate a TON of business, advance my career, enrich the quality of my relationships, get better treatment in service situations, and consistently attract more of what I want – opportunities, friendship, faith and love. With this concept, I have gained happiness, credibility, money, feelings of self-worth, and best of all, a sense of contribution to mankind. Ask anyone who knows me: I am not a boaster, but if something really works, I can't shut up about it. I'll call you at 3am if I think it's good! If I see a good movie, I want everyone to know about it! I bet you're the same way. I don't want to keep what's good to myself; I want others to share and benefit from the experience. That's why I have written this book.

The best news for you is that whatever industry you are in, whatever position you hold – whether it be as a teacher, CEO of a Fortune 500 company, an Elvis impersonator, receptionist, pipe fitter, tech rep, cashier, flight attendant, shrimpin' boat captain, whatever – ***this concept is like an employee that will work for you and reward you in life –personally*** *and professionally - over and over again.*

Let me be straightforward in saying that I don't claim to be a know-it-all. I am of the belief that we can learn from each other. Life is a classroom and it is always in session. What I am sharing is simply what has proven to be useful in my own life, and I believe will be for anyone willing to put it into action. Like many of my incredible mentors, I have read hundreds of books on success, leadership, customer service, sales, etc. *(No kidding!)* I have so many books that I've run out of room for them; they fill up bins and bins in my garage. My point is that my credibility comes through years of persistence and putting this concept into practice. It's been tested and proven to work.

What's interesting is that today more than ever, it seems like everyone is in "search mode." We are always in search of the next thing that can change how we feel, live, attract, overcome, achieve and expand our business. While in "search mode," it's easy to forget the simple fundamentals that are timeless and priceless to building a life of meaning. *Within us all are unique, creative and special abilities that, if used correctly, can produce greatness (more of what we want).*

The experience I'm about to share revealed that truth to me. I have to be honest, it is hard to sit down and read a 300-page book cover to cover. I want and try to all the time, but where the spirit is willing, the flesh is weak. My lifestyle is busy – I travel a lot and you will read about <u>several</u> of my travel experiences, of which I love to share. I understand that you may be busy too. That's why I have kept this book short, quick and to the point. Around my house, I call it A.D.D. friendly! *(I have A.D.D. and one thing A.D.D. ers will do in reading a book is look to see how long a chapter is before they read it.)* I want you to get the most from this book... So if you can, I'd like you to imagine that you and I are meeting up for a cup of coffee at our favorite coffee shop – Earl's Cafe. We'll do this for the next week. We both have a lot to do and the coffee shop gets pretty crowded after 8:30a.m., so we can only meet for about 10 to 15 minutes a day. In that time, I'll share my experience and the lessons it taught me. What you do with it... is entirely up to you. Let's begin...

*"It's not what you've got,
it's what you use that
makes a difference."*

Zig Ziglar

Who Put A Lizard in My Lasagna?

*The things you do for yourself are gone
when you are gone, but the things you
do for others remain as your legacy.*

I had just moved into my one-bedroom apartment. What a monumental moment, to finally have a place to call my own! I was king of the castle, lord of the manor and so broke I could only afford inflatable furniture. It wasn't an easy journey to get to this place. I had lost a large business to a fire, was broke, in debt and became very depressed. Because of my circumstances, I didn't have anywhere to live for a long time, so I stayed with family and often slept on the floor – in the living room or wherever. Eventually, I began to rebuild my life in a positive way. I used the best of who I was to create the best of what I wanted, which I will explain in more detail as we go further. Suffice it to say, at this point in my life, moving into my first one-bedroom apartment was a huge deal.

Still, I didn't have enough money left over for the

so-called essentials like laundry detergent, furniture that didn't require a blow-up pump, or very healthy food. It was always a nice surprise when my mom would visit and have those brown paper grocery bags in both arms. My stomach would leap for joy. I knew those bags were filled with little things to help me. If I was lucky, some of those little things would include leftovers, which I happened to love. One of my favorite leftover dishes was lasagna. If I got lasagna, it was like hitting the jackpot. I reached the end of the rainbow.

My mom and step dad, Andy, would carry in bags filled with valuable items like fruit, popcorn and toilet paper, which you can never have enough of. For me, it was always a highlight when Mom and Andy would stop by and offer a helping hand, then stick around to share in a good laugh.

One particular morning, after I had received a fresh shipment of leftovers, I sat down to enjoy a nice hefty slice of cold lasagna. Little did I know, I was in for an added bonus to my tasty Italian dish. Let me say this, I think it's always slightly disturbing if you find something unexpected in your food that has no place being there... if you get my drift. I think it's probably happened to us all, most likely in the form of that which rhymes with "air, care, bear, chair" (*you get the idea*).

On this one particular day, my mom's heartfelt actions would create a wave of impact that would last for more than a decade and give birth to a concept that would help me build a ton of business, enrich the quality of my relationships, and create a worthwhile legacy.

My mom has always had a great sense of humor. It's part of her legacy. Once when I was 12 years old, my two younger hyperactive A.D.D brothers and I got to go with Mom to the local grocery store. Before we went into the store, we got our normal up-beat motivational speech, *"Okay... LISTEN! Are you listening!? Okay, Mommy loves you very much, but if any of you embarrass me, you will meet God today!"*

As little boys, we knew how to negotiate to get what we wanted. I spoke up and said, "If we are good, can we get candy?" Mom agreed. The last thing we needed was more sugar, but if it kept us on the straight and narrow, Mom was okay with it.

As we stood in line to check out, Mom had forgotten a very important item – milk. She looked at me and said, *"Sam, quickly run and get a gallon of 2% milk."*

I believe in delegation, so I told my smallest brother Chris that if he went to get it, I wouldn't beat him up. He did. I remember Chris, running to the counter with a gallon of 2% milk. And as Murphy's Law would have it, Chris tripped over himself and the milk went flying through the air and exploded all over the floor and all over the other customers waiting in line. (If you've never seen a gallon of milk explode, it's worth the $2.89 to find out. It's pretty entertaining.)

I knew this was more than slightly embarrassing for Mom, because of how red she turned. I looked at my brother Ben and said, *"Looks like we might meet God today."*

Mom began to turn even redder, if that was even possible, and for a moment, as I saw the look on her face, I thought, *"Oh... boy, I don't think she is sending us to heaven."* But Mom surprised us – shocked us more like it. Instead of yelling, flipping out, and sending her three boys on to the afterlife with a boot in the rear, she began to laugh hysterically. And I mean, she laughed hard. If she was drinking the milk, it would have come through her nose.

Instead of seeing the situation as negative, she transformed the experience into something better. She found the lighter side, an act which can be a very important choice.

My brothers and I also began to laugh.

Those who had milk on them didn't share the same sentiment, but we continued to laugh. We didn't even care that management enthusiastically helped us out of the store.

That was a defining moment for me. Mom demonstrated that sometimes the milk is going to spill in life (and boy oh boy, will it spill), but it's still okay to laugh and recognize the lighter side. It's not what happens to you, but how you respond to what happens to you that determines the outcome. It's okay to be a little silly every now and then. That's a natural and healthy response. There is value to that ability. It can be used as an expression of encouragement or love. I know this, because at a time when I really needed encouragement as fuel to keep rebuilding my life and pursuing new dreams, my family stepped up and helped me keep perspective.

As I sat down to indulge in cold leftover lasagna, I rolled back the tin foil, and to my surprise, atop the lasagna was a 3-4 inch long LIZARD! My first thought was, *"My God! My mom cooked a lizard into the lasagna – that's sick!"* Then I pulled it off the pasta dish and discovered it was a plastic lizard! It had a long tail and a silly looking grin. As I slowly pulled the toy lizard off the lasagna, my thought was,

"Who put a lizard in my lasagna? Why? Can I still eat the lasagna – is it still edible?"

This sparked my curiosity, so I called Mom (*collect of course*) and asked, *"Mom, did you put a lizard in the lasagna?"*

Laughing, she said, *"I did!"*

"Why did you do that?"

"Because I thought it would be funny! Did you laugh?"

"I did!"

"Then it worked!"

Oddly enough, it really made my day. It lifted my spirit. I sat there eating lasagna with my new lizard friend. He quickly became the apartment mascot. I didn't think much of it at first, but then it hit me. My mom was being silly, so why not return the favor and create the same unique experience for her? I knew she would get a kick out of it, so my mission was to return the lizard experience, by carefully putting the lizard in her shower.

A few hours later, I got the call, *"Sam, did you put that lizard in my shower?!"*

Laughing, I said, *"I did! Did you laugh?"*

"I did!"

"Then it worked!"

I thought about how fun it was to do that and in my mind thought we were done with the lizard. We had our fun, now it was over, time to plan for our holiday family pranks.

But Mom became like **Frankenstein**. She gave the lizard a life. She somehow snuck it back into my apartment for me to find again.

Now it was really getting funny. Again, I returned the prank, and it kept going back and forth.

For more than a decade, that lizard has seen more hidden and unique places than you can possibly imagine. One time, I actually took the experience a little too far. I "upgraded" our reptilian friend with a different model. Let's just say it was larger than an NFL football and quite realistic looking. It was something that might jump out at you in a horror film. So I decided to put it in my mom's toilet. I put the lid down and thought to myself, *"If this doesn't get a good reaction, I don't know what will."*

A few hours later, I got the much anticipated phone call.

"Sam, did you put that demon in my toilet?!"

Not the exact response I was looking for. Hesitantly, I admitted, *"I did! Ahhh... Did you laugh?"*

"No, but the paramedics did!"

It backfired just a little, but at least it made someone laugh.

Apparently the size, look and location of where you put a toy lizard will determine how funny it will be.

Sometimes it takes me a while to get things, but over the years, I slowly began to find valuable lessons in the lizard experience. I began to draw upon the lizard experience and apply it to important areas of my life and the results I've gotten have been phenomenal!

So how does the "Lizard Experience" apply to your life and profession? What value is it to you? Your gonna find out in a minute, but it might be hard to grasp because of its simplicity. It's almost so simple that some may not be able to comprehend it. It's something we can all do, and a toy lizard isn't even required to make it happen. You already have the means within you. ***The concept of the lizard experience is simply using the best of what you have to create the best of what you want.*** Let's explore how….

The Lizard ...
Creates Memorable Experiences

*A memorable experience lives as
a story in the minds of others...a
story they will share with others.*

The day was cold and rainy in Duluth, Minnesota. So was my attitude. I was feeling a bit stressed. I was running late and trying to get a cab to the airport. I finally hailed a cab, and off we headed.

However, I noticed something moving in the back window area behind me. Not thinking much of it, I looked over my shoulder and, I kid you not, it was a three-pound rat! I'm not sure if I screamed or not (I don't think I would admit it if I had), but I did jump. I asked the cab driver if he knew he had a rat in his car. He started laughing really loud and said with an accent I couldn't quite distinguish, *"Dat's no rat! Dat is a Chihuahua."*

I relaxed a bit, got a half smile and said with a sigh of relief, *"Are you sure about that? It looks like a huge rat."*

The cabby said the dog was old, but still full of

life. Then the ride got a little more interesting. He looked in the rearview mirror and said, *"Hey... Let him licka your face!"*

At this point, I wasn't really feeling comfortable with the suggestion. *"Ummmmm... Why should I let him lick my face?"* I asked.

"Because it makes you feel SOOOOOO good!"

"Oh boy!"

I was reluctant at first and didn't feel like having what I thought was a rat lick my face. But I agreed. The balding dog jumped into my lap, got up on his hind legs and began to lick my face with great enthusiasm. At first, I was somewhat resistant to the treatment. But then, the experience began to transform my attitude. The cabby laughed even more, *"I told you; doesn't it make you feel good?!"*

It actually did feel pretty good. By the time I got to the airport, I was practically licking the dog back! When I got out of the cab, I felt incredible. The experience had changed my mood and outlook for the day.

There are perhaps a hundred cabs in the Duluth area, but when I go back, I don't want just any cab service. I want the one that created an experience worth returning to. I want the one with the lickin' *Chihuahua*. That cabby got a great tip and a customer who was excited to return. He used the best of what he had (a loving dog) to create the best of what he wanted (more business and a loyal customer).

This is the basic premise behind the lizard experience. It's using the best of what you have, wherever you are, and applying it to whatever you do. We are all capable of creating a lizard experience for others.

If there is one thing that builds business or kills it, it's the experience that is created for the customer. Whenever I ask my audiences if they have a bad customer service story, just about every hand goes up in the air. People look frustrated and angry when they tell these stories, as you would expect. But then I ask if anyone has a good service story, and very few hands go up, even though I can see they are trying to recall one. Why is this?

Finding a good service experience these days is like finding a needle in a haystack. Call any company in the yellow pages and see how the person on the other end answers the phone. Walk into any store or business and see what kind of treatment you get. I've come to learn that people who create poor experiences do so because they either don't care, are lazy, hate what they do, let their emotional issues get in the way, or simply just don't get it. I honestly think most people just don't get it.

Either you "get it" or you don't; **the experience you create for others determines what experiences and rewards you will attract and invite into your life.** Hey, for those of you wondering, this isn't new age stuff; it's just good common sense. If you smile at enough people, odds are in your favor you will invite and attract smiles back at you. If you frown at enough people, expect the same in return.

I had one person ask me, *"How can I move forward if I am in a dead-end job with negative people who I can't stand?"*

This describes a lot of people. So what can you do? The key is you have to take on a different mental perspective of your situation. If you rely on this as your source of income and need it to be responsible for bills and such, you have to rethink your mental outlook. Truth is - it is what it is - but some might call it reframing the situation. It's much easier said than done, but a necessity to progress through your situation at hand. Business philosopher Jim Rohn says, *"Don't ask 'what am I getting?,' but instead ask 'what I am becoming?' Because who you become is what you will attract."*

Who you become determines if your value increases or decreases in the working world. I won't lie; I have had a ton of jobs that I hated, but I used them as opportunities to learn, grow and move forward. I have cleaned toilets, washed floors and dishes, delivered newspapers, worked on straight commission and in door-to-door sales, mowed lawns, loaded trucks, worked at a gas station, painted, worked as a copy boy, and answered phones. I worked alongside some of the most negative people and am pretty sure I worked for some supervisors related to Satan.

However, I progressed when my perspective switch went from those jobs using me, to me using them - to learn, grow, and become more valuable in the work force. I watched people in leadership roles and observed what worked for them and what didn't. I placed an expectation upon my life like a farmer does on the seeds he plants. I knew I was going to advance forward at some time, but I needed to learn and make the most of what I had and where I was. Is it easy? Not at all. But if you don't care, are lazy, and complain about how bad the work environment is, then you will see yourself go nowhere - fast. I understand that when you work in a culture that isn't empowering or supportive, it's a mental fight to stay positive. But is there really any benefit to complaining about conditions and people you can't change? The only thing you can change - always - is you. Wherever you are, the key is to get better where you are, and then you will notice that you will begin to move in new directions. Positive changes will happen for you.

It doesn't matter where you fall in the ranks of what you do, we all have a special signature within us that we can stamp onto what we do. That signature is like the lizard and it can make an impact. Inspirational speaker Barbara Glanz says, *"Great service comes from the heart."* My translation of this is, *"Great experiences come from the heart, mind and soul."*

It was the day after New Year's, and I went to the big and tall men's shop to pick up a new coat. The gal working there was in good spirits, and so I asked, *"Why are you so happy?"*

"Because I have a job!"

Her attitude was reflected in the experience she created for me and the work she did in the store. It was memorable and worth returning to.

We all have a special gift within us that we can add to the experiences we create for others. We can extend that gift to customers, a boss, a stranger, our wife, our kids, our co-workers - basically anyone at any time. Sometimes we need to adjust our perspective a bit to see value in what we do and where we are. The simple adjustment can change the experiences you create for others and the way you do your work.

Lizard Insight

Here is one to **REALLY** think about. It's common sense. It's not something new age, a radical off the wall formula or some kind of a secret; it's just plain and simple common sense.

What you send out, comes back. (*What you use creates what you want...if you use what you have the right way*).

Think about it....

> **If you use (your smile), and you smile at 100 people today, odds are in your favor that you will get a lot of smiles in return.**
>
> **If you frown at 100 people, you will get frowns in return .**

Using the best of who you are to create the best of what you want is simply using what you have right now (*gifts, abilities, ideas, experience, skills, education, resources*) where you are and applying them with your best effort. As you are consistent at this, **PROGRESS** takes over and you begin to create and move towards the best of what you want.

The Lizard....
Generates a Ton of Business

How do you create a ton of business?

*Simple: Create an experience
worth returning to.*

I was talking with a few alumni students backstage before a talk at Palmer College of Chiropractic, and was asked about my opinion on what it takes to build a successful business. I told them hands down, *it's the experience we create for customers.*

**You either create something worth
returning to or something they will
run from. It's just that simple.**

If you are ever in the Cleveland airport and need your shoes polished, Mr. Shine creates an incredible experience. As soon as you sit down, the guy working there will offer you something to read. As he cleans your shoes, he incorporates a bit of entertainment into the experience. Mr. Shine will share something

33

positive with you, and when you're done, he says, *"Come on back and see us again!"*

Mr. Shine gets it! He knows how to create a ton of business with the best of who he is and what he has. Whenever I go through Cleveland, I make sure I've got on dirty shoes, because I want the Mr. Shine experience. I walk away with a smile and a pep in my step!

Not only does the "Lizard Experience" help to generate more business, it assists in advancing your career. It puts progress and forward motion into your efforts. You won't be able to stay where you are. You are going to move onward and upward.

The other way, and not my ideal option, to build a ton of business is to watch and learn from those who don't seem to get it. My brother Chris and I once came across a type of person you may be familiar with. We needed to get a camera at a well known electronics store. When we got up to the counter, the teenage girl working the register didn't look at us or even say a simple howdy do. She grabbed the item, threw it in the bag, and looked over the register to say how much the item was. She then looked over her shoulder and started talking to someone else about something else. Her expression was tired, not connected to what she was doing, and I kind of got the impression she couldn't care less who we were (current revenue.. potential future revenue... hint, hint). We are what creates that thing you desire every so often... a paycheck!

Let me ask this:

- Did she make her company look good?
- Would you hire her to do work for you?
- Do you think her actions deserve a raise or advancement?
- Did she create an experience worth returning to?

No. No. No and... NO! The answers are simple.

You might be thinking, "WOW, Sam... *I do know her! She rang me up once too!*" I've got news for you... She is everywhere. She just looks different depending on where you go. It might be a he or she, old or young. Sometimes she is every place you want to be, and that's just not good business.

So, how do you change the experience? Let's find out...

"Success is not the key to happiness.

Happiness is the key to success.

If you love what you are doing, you will be successful."

Albert Schweitzer

10 Essential Ways to Use the Best of Who You Are

You can't aim for success and expect success when you deliver failure.

Ask yourself, what can you do to improve the quality of experiences for others? I have listed 10 top-shelf ways to create positive memorable experiences for others. These simple ideas emphasize a personal touch that creates a connection with others. As a result, the impact is a memorable experience. **Here they are.....**

1. Listen with your eyes.

A little girl was excited to share the events of the day with her momma. But Momma was busy trying to make made dinner at the same time she listened.

The little girl said, *"Momma, I need you to listen."*

She acknowledged the little girl, *"Honey, I am listening."*

"No, Momma, I need you to listen with your eyes."

Look people in the eyes and let them know they have your attention.

2. BEFORE YOU TAKE CENTER STAGE, GET YOUR ATTITUDE RIGHT.

The essence of every experience starts with our attitude. I was once waiting to get a haircut. The woman who was cutting hair was talking on the phone, and I noticed she began to get really mad. She hung up the phone and yelled, *"I HATE MEN!"* Her next words were, *"WHO'S NEXT?!?"*

My immediate thought was, *"Our Father who art in heaven…"*

Her attitude wasn't right and it got in the way of being great. I could feel her tension with each cut. It created a lousy experience for me and the other men waiting to get their hair cut. I never saw so many eyes that looked like they were going to pop out. I never went back and I still have the baseball cap I bought after the haircut (no joke!).

If your attitude is not right, it doesn't matter how great, talented or smart you are. It doesn't matter how much experience or education you have; the wrong attitude working through you only hurts yourself and others. It makes for a poor experience. Attitude is an asset we have that we can use to create the best of what we want. The wrong attitude is like bad breath - it works against you. Ever been around someone with bad breath? Did you feel like sticking around? Probably not.

Remember, your attitude is your choice. It's always at work – working *for* you or *against* you – and you determine which. Having a good attitude won't eliminate adversity and the feelings that come with it, but it sure helps move through it faster.

If you want to expand your company, move up, attract new customers, retain current customers, etc. the answer is simple. **Enrich the quality of your attitude. People feel it, see it and remember it.** It comes through in how you answer the phone, do your work, treat co-workers, customers, etc... Only you know how you can best enrich the experience for others. It starts with your attitude – ask yourself if your attitude is working for you or against you. What can you do to improve the quality of your attitude?

3. SMILE.

*"If you see someone without a
smile, give them one of yours."*

Jacquelinemae Rudd

A woman and I were taking the elevator up. When we stopped at her floor, the doors opened. She turned before she got off, smiled at me, and said, *"You have a great day!"*

I was pleasantly surprised that a stranger would take the time to smile at me and wish me well. I gladly smiled back, and when I got off at my floor with a smile still intact, I turned back and said, "You have a good day!" Now there was no one on there anymore, but it just felt right to do… and good. Smiles do work. They are simple, not expensive at all and surprisingly effective. Just make sure you brush your teeth first.

Think of an experience that made you smile or impacted your life and then duplicate it for others. A smile is the fastest way to create a memorable experience and connection with someone else.

4. TAKE THE BEST OF WHO YOU ARE AND APPLY IT TO WHAT YOU DO.

*"Do what you can with what
you have, where you are."*

Theodore Roosevelt

I truly believe we get promoted and advance forward in life when we take the best of who we are and apply it to what we do. What this means is, don't complain about what you don't have or what you wish was different. Step up and play the cards you were dealt. Here is a quote that was sent to me that really sums up this point,

*"You can't change the level of
your talent/ability, but you can
change the level of your effort."*

James Blake, professional tennis player

Do an inventory of what your strengths are and how you can use your effort to apply them. Are you dependable, honest, consistent, open-minded, respectful, teachable, a team player, energetic, hard working, caring…?

There are so many ways you can apply this principle. I used to drive an '82 Buick Regal and the year was far from 1982. It wasn't the most attractive car, but instead of complaining (which this car presented every opportunity to do), I did the best I could with what I had. I kept the inside clean by throwing out all of the White Castle boxes. I washed the car regularly and did what was necessary and responsible toward keeping a car running. As a result, something inside of me eventually said, *"Sam, you were a good steward with the resources you had, and now you are financially and deservedly ready to advance."* I felt deserving of a new car and that's just what I got.

Some might argue, *"Well, if you wanted a new car, you could have gotten one – no matter what shape your last car was in."* True, but when I got the new car, **I felt deserving of it because I had made the best of what I had. That made it more rewarding.** I used the best of what I had to create the best of what I wanted.

5. BE NICE.

"Your rewards in life are in direct proportion to your service."

Earl Nightingale

Isn't it nice when people treat you with kindness? It's a warm feeling. If you call our company, chances are you will hear a very sweet and pleasant voice answer your call. That voice belongs to my Program Coordinator, Michelle. Some days, because of the call volume we get, you may get our voicemail, but it's Michelle's voice. No matter how many calls we get each day, her pleasant voice never changes.

When I first hired her, before we did any kind of formal training, I told her I wanted our company members to always be nice to clients, even if they were not nice back to us. I wanted people to remember how nice it was to work with us. Michelle's story is a testimony to how to build a ton of business and attract the success you desire.

What is extra special about Michelle is that after you talk with her, you literally feel like you have made a new friend. You don't feel like you've just chatted with a difficult person or someone who is in a rush or too busy to pay attention. What's exciting is that when I show up to my speaking engagements, the number one comment I get over and over is, *"Michelle was the absolute best to work with. We've worked with a lot of speakers, but we have never worked with anyone like Michelle. She was so nice!"*

Michelle understands that the experience we create for others starts with her. As a result, Michelle has become a huge success within our organization. She now has ownership in something that rewards her family and herself. Hard work and kindness do pay dividends.

People ask me time and time again, how do you build a ton of business? Is it all marketing? We use marketing to create awareness, but the best business that pays time and time again is the experience we create. The heart of building our business is simple, *"We create an experience worth returning to."*

Does this mean we are perfect all the time? Not at all. Sometimes we flop. With technology the way it is, so many things can go wrong, and sometimes they do. We have had moments when our voicemails got erased because the system was reset, important emails went to spam and got deleted, book orders got lost in the mail, etc. (You know how it is.) These setbacks can be especially frustrating when your mission is to create an experience worth returning to. Some things happen that you can't control, but you have to roll with it and recover the best you can. When things go wrong, we are very honest about the situation and own our errors. The key is in learning from mistakes. That's what success in business is; it's learning what works and what doesn't, and then consciously doing a lot more of what works.

You might ask, how do we handle those who are not nice? Well, I personally like to prank phone call them at 3a.m. over and over again, and that pretty much solves everything. Okay, not really, but it's fun to think about. Actually, we continue to express kindness and understanding. If someone complains, we thank them for bringing the issue to our attention and then we act diligently to serve their needs. Don't fight back with a difficult client – ever! If there is a fire in the room, you don't try to make it bigger, you act urgently to put it out. If we're talking with someone who is upset, we listen, sympathize, understand and offer options to reconcile and create a solution. It can be difficult at times, because there are moments the customer is not always right. I always stress the importance of using tact and good communication in any case to get back to a common ground where everyone is getting what they want.

Sometimes, people are having a bad day and just need to talk with someone nice to make it all better. You can be that person!

6. OFFER GOOD NEWS! (REPACKAGE THE BAD NEWS.)

"Mr. Glenn, good news… We made a huge mistake on your taxes and we are going to issue you a large refund!"

People love good news, but it's become common to expect bad news (we seem to be used to it). If you want to build a ton of business, learn to give people good news. You ask, *"What if there is no good news?"* Well then, find ways to make a poor situation better. You can do that.

I once called to set up a dental appointment, and the date I requested wasn't open, but the woman on the phone said, *"Good news! There are openings on these days instead. Do any of them work for you, Mr. Glenn?"*

Do you see how she turned the situation around?

Once I checked into a hotel and my room was

not ready (which happens a lot). But this time, I met someone who "gets it." The person behind the counter could have said, *"Your room is not ready, can you come back in a few hours?"* (I've heard this many times). However, this particular hotel offered me some better news, which I thought was refreshing and innovative. *"Mr. Glenn, I am so sorry your room is not ready, but we would like to treat you to lunch and some of the best tasting desserts you will ever have. I don't expect it will be much longer, but if it is, I will let you know and we will do our best to make you comfortable until your room is ready for you."*

Folks, this wasn't a four-star hotel. This was simply someone who understood how to create an experience worth returning to. That's how you build business and positive relationships.

I'll give one last example. I was at the Salt Lake City airport and my flight was delayed for hours until it was finally canceled. I was upset and frustrated because I needed to get to a speaking engagement by the next day. I finally got to the counter to start the rebooking process, and I really didn't know what to expect or what news they would give me. But the woman helping me said, *"I am really sorry about this, but we can get you out first thing in the morning and we are upgrading you to first class."* It wasn't ideally what

I wanted, but she repackaged the information into a good news format.

She could have just said, *"We can't get you out until tomorrow; you're going to have to deal with it. It's not my fault. I don't control the weather."*

She did not do this. Instead, she was sincere and repackaged the bad news into better news.

Think about how, when you are faced with a difficult situation, you might be able to offer information in the form of good news to improve the situation. This may require some creative thinking, but it helps remedy situations that may be out of your control. It might not be the best news to someone, but it doesn't have to be that bad either – it can even be good news! I remember one customer service person who was trying to make a situation better asked me, *"Mr. Glenn, what can we do?"* I responded, *"Make me smile."*

When you offer good news, you are also leading people in their thinking. You are directing traffic in their minds. Instead of presenting information laced with doom and gloom, you repackage it with a positive spin that creates good news feelings.

7. DRESS RIGHT, SMELL RIGHT.

Ever work with someone who smells less-than rosy? I have, and I tried to avoid them at all costs. My Secret Santa gift to that person was Tic Tacs, soap on a rope and a variety of fragrances. Hey, if you stink, how can that help your situation? This lesson can be taken literally as well as figuratively. (Your attitude shouldn't stink, and neither should you!)

You don't get a second chance to make a first impression. Dress the part and be the part. I recently had dinner with a couple and was informed by the husband that he worked as a mechanic for more than 25 years. The most impressive part about his story was when he told us that he wore a white shirt and tie every day. I asked him, *"Didn't you ever get dirty?"*

"Sure, but with enough experience you learn how to stay clean," he said. *"Plus, it gave customers confidence in the person taking care of their auto. It wasn't required to wear a shirt and tie, but I did it and it created an experience of excellence for the customer and for me."*

I could relate to his story. Just after I graduated from high school, I got a job working at a gas station near my house. The required uniforms were awful-looking red smocks. They had unidentified and disgusting stains on them and didn't look attractive. I decided to take initiative; I wore a nice shirt and tie to work instead. Let me point out, I hate wearing ties. My buddies at Men's Warehouse always try to sell them to me, but I am just not a tie guy. However, for this job, I wanted to look professional and presentable, even if I was pumping gas, cleaning bathrooms, and working the register. Being dressed up, I actually felt more confident and important. Most customers actually thought I was the manager, and were surprised to find out I wasn't. In fact, I looked better than the manager. I remember some regional executives stopped in our shop one day and were so impressed with my efforts, they approached me about being a manager.

8. BE HONEST.

Have you ever had someone take advantage of you? I think we all have at some point. It doesn't feel good or sit well within us. Using manipulation to get what you want is dishonest and wrong. People get hurt.

Someone close to me purchased a car on eBay a few years back. She researched it, used CARFAX to check its history, and saw that everything checked out. It was a good deal. She flew to Ohio to pick it up, and a short time later when she went to trade it in, she discovered that the car had been in a terrible accident with the first owner. The dealership dishonestly put the incorrect VIN number on the eBay site to conceal the car's history. This is a case of manipulating people to get ahead. But in reality, do dishonest people actually get ahead? No, they don't. I happen to believe in karma, and that it comes back to bite them like a snake with severe anger management problems.

Remember to be real with people. Trust is a bridge to success. Studies show that what keeps people from buying is a lack of trust. I know personally, if I get a bad vibe from someone that says, *"They're taking me for all I've got,"* I won't buy.

9. PUT A CHERRY ON TOP!

You don't have to be perfect,
but you can choose to be great.

This concept is all about adding something a little "extra special" to your efforts. Do something that stands out. Think about how some hotels put chocolates on your pillow. When I stayed at the Hershey Park Hotel, I was surrounded by so much chocolate that I had to keep pinching myself to make sure it was real. I actually fell asleep with a chocolate bar in my hand. When I woke up, the chocolate had melted all over me *and* the sheets. I called down to get new sheets. The woman asked if everything was okay, and I said, *"Yes, you guys put a chocolate bar on my pillow and I was so excited I fell asleep with it. The chocolate melted and got all over the place!"*

The woman apologized. In good humor, I said *"No.. No... It's okay. I ate most of what seemed still edible. I didn't want it to go to waste."* (I might have freaked her out at this point, but come on – it's chocolate!).

We all have something "extra special" that we can bring to a situation. It can be unique and simple, but best of all, it's our personal signature on the experience we create for others. When my brothers and I were in junior high, our parents would leave us a few chores to do before they got home from work. Sure, we weren't always excited about chores, but every once in a blue moon there was that instance when we would decide to add something "extra special," and deep-clean the house, make the dinner (i.e., order a pizza!), mow the yard, or find another way to make it a little more pleasant and stress-free for them to come home. And they sure appreciated it.

What's your something extra? Think about your "extra special" signature and apply it to your efforts.

10. DISCOVER YOUR UNIQUENESS AND USE IT IN A POSITIVE WAY.

Choose to be the best version of yourself,
not a second rate version of someone else.

I learned this lesson from my friend Larry Winget, who is also a best-selling author of several books including his latest, <u>You're Broke Because You Want to Be Broke</u>. I had the chance to attend one of Larry's meetings on how to improve a speaking career. During lunch, as I visited with Larry about my career, he gave me these wise words: *"Discover what is unique about you and exploit it. Market it like crazy. Don't try to be like me or anyone else. Be your uniqueness."*

He is right. Many times people try to copycat others. There is a perception that if we copy them, we will feel more valuable and reach the same level of success. Modeling success is modeling actions. It's not losing yourself or your own personal brand. I remember hearing a speaker tell one of my stories and at first I thought, am I Sam Glenn or is he? Is he pretending he is me? Why would he take my story and make it his own? It was wrong and he got called out on it, which turned out to be very embarrassing for him.

The lesson to grasp is this: the fastest way to the bottom of the success ladder is to be something or someone you are not. **The purpose of this book is to get you to recognize your own personal value – right where you are.** Hey, I know it's sometimes easier to see it in others, but stop it! Begin to recognize your own value and then apply it. You don't have to be perfect to get going in life, just begin with who you are, where you are and let progress do its part.

It's not about what you don't have; it's about how you use what you do have. It's not about comparing yourself to others or wishing upon a star that things were different. You have something unique and valuable about you, and you should not underestimate that. You have gifts, abilities, insights, so why not use them to your advantage? The more you use them, the more developed you become. Don't spend valuable time dwelling on what you don't have, or what's a weakness, but rather put the same energy into recognizing your uniqueness and strengths. Take a moment to think of what is unique about you. What is your personal signature? Is it humor? Attitude? Heart? Is it the way you walk into a room? (*"Hey everyone!"*) Or is it how you clear a room? If you take the time to consider this question, you will realize the answer.

I get bored leaving normal voicemails. (*"Hi this is Sam. Call me."*) I like to spice it up with something extra special (my own personal uniqueness). I want my voicemails to make people laugh, smile, and have a better day. And they do... in a humorous and dysfunctional way! I know people who have saved my voice messages for years.

Again, don't try to be someone you're not. That's how you bomb on the stage of life. If you had the opportunity to buy an original piece of art or a copy, which would you prefer? Of course the original. So be the best original you can be. Learn from others, study successful actions, but hold onto your unique identity.

"If a man practices doing things for other people until it becomes so much a habit that he is unconscious of it, all of the good forces of the universe line up behind him and whatever he undertakes to do."

Bruce Barton

10 Fast Ideas for Enriching the Quality of Your Experiences With Others:

1. Do what you say you will do in the time you say you will do it.

2. Nobody gives a hoot about your policies, so if you've got them, you don't need to talk about them. They are there to guide you, not for you to use to explain away why someone is not having a good experience.

3. If you make a mistake, own it, fix it, learn from it and move on.

4. Use good manners – respect is essential to great experiences.

5. Treat others how you wish to be treated.

6. Find a way to make people happy. Never tell someone that there is nothing you can do. Don't speak down to them either. They don't want to hear negatives; that only makes the situation worse. Grow some wings and become an eagle. Do what ducks won't. Eagles are problem solvers. They take action on your behalf. Ducks become part of the problem. They are lazy, uncaring and lack vision to find

solutions. Which are you? You are either part of the problem or part of the solution. It's that simple.

7. Don't take complaints personally. If someone is upset, be empathetic and let them vent. Don't interrupt, fight back or blame someone else. It's easy to get reactive when people are giving you a negative piece of their mind. See the instance as your personal opportunity to improve their experience. Allow them to get negative information – or what I like to call the toxins – out, and then address these people in a way that lets them know you are not against them, but on their side.

8. Great experiences don't come from a book; they come from your heart, mind and soul. Add your own personal and unique touch to what you do.

9. Little things go a long way. Do them.

10. Be an encourager, not a discourager. Use positive words. Tell people how grateful you are for them. Compliment them. Make them feel important. Recognize and reward instantly, and publicly.

As long as you ask this question,

"Is there anything I can I do for you?"

You will always have work, you will always have friends and you will always make a difference.

The Lizard ...
Creates a Positive "Mild"
Distraction

What is a positive "mild" distraction?
It is a mental interruption that breaks
our current mental patterns and assists
us in regaining a positive perspective
on what's important and what's not.

Have you ever been so busy, stressed out and overwhelmed that you forgot something important? It's not funny, but it kinda is when you hear those stories about the families that took off down the road and about five miles later realized, *"We forgot the kids!"*

Life has a way of getting unbalanced, and when things cloud our thoughts, we need a positive, "mild" distraction that gets us off the wrong mental track and back to one that works in our favor.

I remember being in a mad rush to get to the airport. However, I could not find my car keys and looked everywhere. I was exhausted at the very thought of sitting in Chicago traffic – it's all I could think about, and it began to make my stress level rise. I was sweating Tabasco sauce and became a bit irritable. And to top it off, I was hungry. My blood sugar was low. I think you know that when you are stressed or hungry, your attitude can turn to the dark side really fast. When your attitude goes south, so does your perspective on what's happening around you. **When you lose perspective, you lose the ability to think right and act right.**

I finally found my keys. As I was putting on my shoes, my right foot would not go all the way in. Something was causing an obstruction. At first I thought, *"What now?"* I reached in and pulled out "The Lizard." There he was again, grinning at me! Despite being in such a rush, stressed out, and hungry, the lizard brought me back to a healthy perspective. My sanity was restored. A smile surfaced and the stress slowly began to dissolve. The lizard served as a positive "mild" distraction and as a result, I lightened up, relaxed and got back into the moment, but with a different mental state.

Whenever I find that lizard, it reminds me, *"Each situation is what I decide to make of it."*

So you ask, what if things are going crazy and there isn't a lizard in my shoe to break my mental state?

Then you plan your positive "mild" distractions. The key to keeping a positive perspective is to create positive "mild" distractions for yourself so that when life gets out of sorts, you have something that restores your best attitude. Maybe it's putting up a positive quote on the white board or having a picture of you and a beloved friend on your desk. Take a walk. Jump in the shower. Go to the puppy store and play with puppies. Go bowling. Watch a funny movie. Eat some cheese… (I do.) Do anything that soothes you and releases you from your stresses. I enjoy listening to relaxing jazz. I'll turn on my iPod and just breathe, relax and let go. Letting go of the stress allows me to use my mind in more productive ways.

To be successful and progress towards what you want in life, your mind has got to be right. You cannot walk right, and think left. It doesn't work. A hot head will only burn you and others. The key is thinking ahead and planning a few positive "mild" distractions that you know will cool you down, relax your tense thinking, and get you back on track to a healthy state of mind. It's important to recognize that doing something in excess – like over eating, taking up residence on the couch, watching too much TV, or abusing certain substances, can have a counter effect in helping you get back to your most effective mental state. A positive "mild" distraction is not a quick fix to a situation, or a fleeing technique. Just the opposite, it enables you to get back to your best mindset.

I had one woman tell me how one of her co-workers sometimes gets crazy-upset and just wants to argue about why things are not different than they are. When she is like this, she is not open to new ideas, suggestions or finding a common ground. Before you know it, an hour has passed, nothing is resolved and everyone is feeling mentally worn out.

I suggested a positive "mild" distraction. The next time she starts going off and you feel that things are not productive or going in a positive direction, you need to kindly interrupt her and say, *"I need a five-minute break,"* or *"I need to use the rest room."* Take about 10 minutes and just walk away from the fire for a bit. Let it simmer down and see if things are a bit better when you return.

She tried this and told me it worked!

But, when she tried it again, the other person said, "No… We need to talk about this now; we don't have five minutes to spare."

She told me that she then thought on her feet and

told the woman, "No, I still think we need to take a break before continuing this discussion. I didn't want to say anything, but here are some Tic Tacs. Be back in five!"

Now she says that anytime she asks for that five-minute break, the woman doesn't argue. Since she thinks her breath might stink, she is more than okay with it! WOW! That's bold, but it worked for her.

Health experts tell us when we find ourselves getting worked up, we should count to 10. Why is this? By doing so, it distracts the mind from focusing on the situation at hand. It gives you 10 seconds to not feed the fire with more negative thinking. It allows you to simmer. If you are like me, you can greatly benefit from thinking ahead by pre-planning a variety of positive "mild" distractions. (I actually have Play-do in my desk drawer. Sometimes I pull it out and connect with my inner child. People see the Play-do and ask if I have kids and I tell them… No, it's mine. Odd looks again, but this positive "mild" distraction works for me. What will work for you?

The Lizard ...
Creates Empowering Enthusiasm

"Enthusiasm releases the drive to carry you over obstacles and adds significance to all you do."

Norman Vincent Peale

"Enthusiasm is the yeast that raises the dough."

Paul J. Meyer

Every time I hide the lizard for mom to find, there is enthusiasm in my efforts. I am excited about what I am doing and as a result I do it well. **That's what enthusiasm does; it puts positive energy into your actions.** When you have enthusiasm, you give your best. You want to give your best. Enthusiasm can be felt by others and is contagious. The great thing about enthusiasm is it either adds incredible value to the experiences you create or takes away for lack of.

I have made some amazing discoveries about

this wonderful attitude trait. I think it's become overlooked and underestimated, which is sad, because it packs so much life, inspiration and energy. I have discovered that enthusiasm is a lifeline to achieving consistent success. I honestly believe that "real success" does not exist without enthusiasm. When you have enthusiasm, you see a greater value in yourself and your efforts. A job is no longer just a job, but rather it becomes an opportunity.

Years ago, I got involved with a group that worked in helping teenagers with character issues. I was to be an intern at a camp for two months. I was excited... until they assigned the jobs for the summer. I was given the wonderful duty of cleaning bathrooms. Let's be real here, there is nothing wonderful about cleaning bathrooms on a campground. There were close to 40-plus toilets on that campground. Let me ask you something; if someone asks you to clean the toilet at home or the office, do you get excited about it? NO WAY! I had 40 of them! I became so negative and doubted my role in making a difference. I personalized the situation in a negative way and as a result, I didn't give my best. In fact, I did an awful job – the minimum to get by. I kept thinking, *"I am much more than a toilet cleaner! Who do they think they are to make me do this? Why did they make me do this?*

Do I have toilet cleaner man written on my forehead? I want to go home!!"

I almost did. I hit my breaking point with this duty and so I rode my pride and high horse all the way to the camp director's office to quit and discuss how cleaning toilets isn't a real significant way to make a difference! There are bigger things that make a difference.

When I was done venting, he calmly explained to me a different perspective to the situation that I could not see because of the black cloud hovering over my attitude.

"Sam, everything we do here makes a difference. Imagine what those bathrooms would look like if you didn't clean them. You have an opportunity to contribute to the big picture here. What you do matters and is important. Your efforts are valued. But if you are not giving your best, you are selling yourself and others short. The little things make a big difference, Sam. You can choose to do the little things big and be a difference maker or you can choose to do get by on the wrong attitude and be an average maker. What's it going to be?"

That mental switch helped restore a sense of value in who I was and what I was doing.

Sometimes we lose sight of the big picture in the

midst of doing the little things, and as a result, it's those little things that hold the big picture together.

I developed a renewed outlook for my toilet cleaning job. I no longer viewed it as me fighting against 40 toilet beasts or something negative, but I chose to be a positive contribution to the big picture. And in making that choice, I had a revived sense of enthusiasm. As a result, it could be seen in my work, and that made me a difference maker, not an average maker. My enthusiasm moved me forward, where my lack thereof had only kept me in a dark place with no hope of progress.

It's not about position, experience, rank or skills; it's about being willing to do whatever it takes and applying enthusiasm. It's not so much about what we have to do, but how we do it that makes the difference. I understand that there are moments and certain people that try to steal our enthusiasm, but the more you practice it, the stronger it becomes in your life and the harder it is to shake. Enthusiasm will allow you to have a special kind of vision that negative people won't. It will push you to be excellent, stand out, progress, and make a difference – which ultimately is creating the best of what you want by using the best of who you are.

The Lizard...
Enriches the Quality of Our
Relationships

*"The issue in relationships is not just
how much you love people, but how
much they can feel your love."*

Barbara DeAngelis

Meaningful relationships are strong because of the connection. The lizard has created a deeper connection between my mom and me. When she or I find that lizard, we know we have been remembered by the other person. It's an expression of love. When I find that lizard, I know my mom took special time to think of me.

Remember this statement: meaningful actions create meaningful results. The goal of every relationship should be to get it to a place where it is meaningful. All meaningful relationships require attention. Attention creates connection.

Whatever you give attention to grows and whatever you ignore fades away. When you value your relationships, you take the time to create and strengthen your connections.

For my mom and me, that lizard continues to nurture our relationship. It's a connection.

After one speech, a very nice woman from my audience told me that instead of a lizard, she and her family do the same thing with a colorful sock. The sock bonds the family closer together.

One woman took home one of the plastic lizards I give out at the end of my talks. She gave it to her 6-year-old son and shared the story about the lizard experience and how hiding it for someone to find is one way to express love. The next day, when she got to work, she opened her briefcase and there was the lizard. In this small way, her son was showing that he was learning to nurture his relationships by taking time to think of the other person.

Life is empty without meaningful relationships.

The key to the lizard experience is using sincerity to enrich the quality of your relationships. It's not about manipulating others to get what you want. It's about being genuine, authentic and real. Meaningful relationships aren't about what you get, but rather about what you contribute. Too often, the mentality is *"What am I getting out of this?"*

The pursuit of deeper relationships is not about what you get, but rather who are you becoming. Time expressed through understanding, love, forgiveness, patience, humor and thoughtfulness is what deepens relationships. Our time is always being pressed, but investing time into relationships will only create benefits for you and others. Even if you are in a rush and only have a few minutes, take time to make someone laugh, smile or feel important.

Consider what this father did with his 4-year-old daughter. She was jumping on the bed as Daddy was getting ready for a business trip. She kept asking Daddy to play with her. But Daddy was busy and told her, *"I can't right now, Sweetie... Daddy is in a rush. Maybe later."*

"No, Daddy. Now! I need you now!" The little girl was relentless and kept asking him to play.

Finally, he said, *"If you don't let me get ready, I'm gonna eat your finger."*

The little girl giggled and said, *"No you won't, Daddy!"*

Daddy smiled and said, *"Yes I will."*

Still giggling, the little girl kept jumping up and down, when finally the father reached out in playfulness, grabbed the little girl's finger and said, *"I'm gonna eat it!"*

He jokingly put her finger in his mouth and said, *"Yummy... I ate your finger."*

The little girl, laughing out loud, said, *"No you didn't, Daddy!"*

They both laughed and the father was happy that he had stopped to take that brief moment to make his daughter laugh. It made them both feel good.

But suddenly, his daughter stopped laughing. She looked puzzled and stared at the finger that was in her daddy's mouth. He asked the little girl, *"What's wrong, Honey?"*

"Daddy, I know you didn't eat my finger, but I think you ate my booger!"

Time is a big word when it comes to relationships. I am no relationship expert, but one thing I do know for sure is we can't go through life alone. We cannot succeed alone. Without meaningful relationships, it doesn't matter what we achieve. If we don't have people to share it with, life is meaningless.

One way I like to build positive relationships is

by meeting up with friends over breakfast at our favorite cafe. I keep a pretty busy schedule, but when I get a free moment and am in town, I like to enjoy a nice cup of coffee, two eggs scrambled, a side of bacon, and the company of good friends. During that time, we share thoughts, opinions, hardships, encouragements or whatever is going on in our lives. At the end of the meal, when we walk out the door, we walk out full... and not just from the food.

Explore the best of who you are and use it to enrich the quality of your relationships. Perhaps you are good at expressing words of encouragement, offering support, running errands, listening, praying, or donating time or money. There are a lot of things that can be done. What is your relationship strength? What can you do to add some positive value to your relationships?

The Lizard.....
Connects Us with the Lighter
Side of Things

When we feel good, we do good.

*"Find ways to play. We can be
serious about our work without
being serious about ourselves."*

The book, FISH!

The fastest way to feel good is through laughter
produced by good humor. Almost every time I
find the lizard in an unexpected place, it makes me
laugh. It interrupts the normal flow of my day and
offers me something unexpected and humorous. I
embrace that. One time, I pulled out my wallet at
the airport to show my I.D. and there was the lizard
for all to see. It was unexpected for me and the guy
checking my I.D. The guy smiled, looked at me and
said, *"Do you always walk around with a fake lizard in
your wallet?"*

To me, another thing the lizard experience communicates is *"Lighten up!"* If there is one thing we need to do more of it is to lighten up. I am sure you are thinking of someone right now who needs to lighten up. If you can't think of anyone, then someone else reading this might be thinking of you! Laughter makes us feel good and is proven to make us more attractive. If you want to improve your attraction factor, just lighten up a bit. Lightening up doesn't mean standing around the water cooler telling jokes; it means embracing the humor that surrounds you in every day. There is a ton of it going on around you, and it doesn't even have to make sense. It feels so good, so embrace the benefits of it!

I totally understand that there is nothing more frustrating than working or dealing with someone who is over-the-top uptight. They let their ego get in the way and tend to complain and criticize more. They are not fun to be around. So, what can you do about it? For starters, don't be like them. The key to embracing humor is finding ways to unleash your lighter side or reconnect with your inner child. The positive side effects of laughter are that we burn calories, create a tighter stomach, and create a strong connection between us and others, whether they are customers, loved ones, or strangers.

I was talking with a woman at Blue Cross Blue Shield, an organization I really enjoy speaking for. She told me a story about something inspiring that happened to her. She said that the phone had rung but she was still laughing really hard from something her co-worker had just told her. As she picked up the phone, the customer on the other end heard the laughter. The customer said, *"I have been talking with people on the phone all day, but hearing your laughter made my day."*

Laughter has the power to create connections that build business. One of my friends uses humor to attract new customers. He will call and leave this voicemail to get a return call, *"Hello, this is so and so. A priest, a rabbi and a fisherman walk into a bar. If you want to hear the rest of this joke, call me back."* It's hysterical; people actually call him back to get the rest of the joke!

Sharing humor with others is not about being a comedian, but rather about taking a situation and finding the lighter side to it. You can also collect humor and share it with others in a positive way. That's part of the "lizard experience."

THE TOP 7 THINGS TO SAY WHEN CAUGHT DOZING AT YOUR DESK:

1. "They told me at the blood bank this might happen."

2. "This is just a 15-minute power nap like they raved about in the time management course you sent me to."

3. "Whew! Guess I left the top off the White Out. You probably got here just in time."

4. "I wasn't sleeping! I was meditating on the mission statement and envisioning a new paradigm."

5. "I was testing my keyboard for drool resistance."

6. "I was doing a highly specific yoga exercise to relieve work-related stress. Are you discriminatory toward people who practice yoga?"

7. ".....in Jesus' name. Amen."

HUMOR STRENGTHENS CONNECTIONS.

There is nothing like making someone else laugh and knowing that you helped create that moment. One way I use humor is to build a deeper connection with my friends and family. Several years ago, I introduced them all to the comedy style of my favorite comedian, Brian Regan. I am often compared to him, Will Ferrell and someone's weird uncle, so it's a huge honor. I never try to be like anyone but Sam Glenn, but for some reason, people are always matching me up with someone.

If anyone lives the concept of this book, it's Brian. I remember when we first met Brian Regan backstage at Zanies in Vernon Hills, Illinois. I wanted to create a "feel good" experience for my family, so I got everyone tickets to see him. We laughed so hard our stomachs hurt. Someone even peed his pants. *(I just told everyone I spilled my Coke.)*

When the show was over, we sat there a bit and reminisced about how funny it was sitting in the audience because a few short years before, I actually performed on the same stage. I never pursued stand-up, because I just felt my calling was to do what I am doing today. But, it was almost eight years before when I saved a group of wanna-be comedians. I forget the name of the place, but it was pretty much a dive. And the audience was louder than the comedians. It was enough to make you feel uncomfortable for the performers.

A friend asked me if I would go up and say something funny. Being funny on stage and being funny around friends are two DIFFERENT worlds. At first I was resistant. Or better put – SCARED OUT OF MY MIND! I didn't know what to say, so I just used some improv, got up on stage and "surprisingly" rocked the house. When I got off stage, someone handed me a card from Zanies and the next thing you know, I'm onstage performing a not-so-well-thought-out bit.

After Brian's performance, I got up to visit the Zanies manager to see if she remembered me, and surprisingly she did. It had been close to eight years and she still remembered the specific humor I used as well! She and I chatted a bit and then we got to meet Brian. He was so nice and engaging; it was quite impressive. We were fans before we met him, but his performance off stage made us die-hard fans. He created an experience worth returning to, worth telling others about.

Brian is someone who really understands how to use the best of who you are to create the best of what you want. He uses humor, sincerity, and kindness (his gifts and abilities) to create an experience for others. The rewards are happiness, security for his family, purpose, and fulfillment.

This is an example of using the best of who you are and what you have to create the best of what you want. The good news is, we are each entitled to the same things.

DEVELOP HUMOR AWARENESS.

I am always telling my audiences, *"You are your best source of humor."* If you can look at your life in a way that's receptive to joy and humor, you'll be able to recognize some pretty entertaining things.

Years ago, I was in line at Wal-Mart. I only had singles – about 94 of them. (Why? I don't recall. It was all I had at the time.) As I was being rung up, I started counting out $86 in singles to pay for my items. The two women waiting behind me were watching and began to comment, *"Look at all those singles. He must be one of those... you know... dancers that gets paid with singles."*

The other woman quickly chimed in, *"Claire, that's not nice. He might be a pastor of a church."*

I saw this is a great opportunity to use humor. I

turned to them, put on a huge smile and said, *"It's funny you say that; I am actually both!"*

Everyone in that line began laughing. Even the woman working the register.

Sometimes we just need a little humor to improve our mood. The value again is that when we feel better, we do better.

"You don't stop laughing because you grow old; you grow old because you stop laughing."

Michael Prichard

The Lizard...
Challenges You to Be More
Creative

*"The world is but a canvas
to the imagination".*

Henry David Thoreau

For more than a decade, finding new places to hide that lizard to surprise my mom has been a challenge. Both of us have been challenged to think creatively to continue creating an unexpected experience.

Getting what you want with what you have requires being creative – thinking outside the triangle. *(Don't limit yourself to thinking only outside the box. That takes you so far. In order to be more creative, you have to take it another step.)*

We all have the elements of creativity within us. I'm sure the first time you tried to cook, it was a creative experience. The first drawing you ever did as a child had to be creative. We all have the potential for creativity within us; it's an artful expression of who we are. The value of creativity is that it can produce solutions and turn ideas into reality.

Sometimes you have to <u>rethink</u> what you are doing and make some creative modifications. Let me share a few examples. A few days ago, I stopped into one of those quick oil change places. It was "Chicago" cold out. I warmed up in the waiting area next to a television that was turned up so loud, I think it even annoyed the dead. As I was checking emails on my phone, the owner (who I had seen there before) walked out to the main road in front of the shop with an American flag. He then began to wave the flag back and forth for almost 10 minutes. It was an interesting site to behold. I looked at the guy working behind the counter, *"My, he is very patriotic."*

"Yes, but he is trying to wave more business in."

"Really, does he normally do this?"

"Sometimes. I think he might be losing his mind."

I just laughed, but I began thinking about how if the owner wanted to successfully create more business, all he needed to do was use what he had to create the best of what he wanted. He had three customers in the waiting room. He could have walked up, introduced himself, offered us a soft drink, and handed out a coupon for the next time we came in. That was merely my take, but I am sure there were other things he may have been able to do that would have created more of a relationship with his customers than waving that flag by the roadside. What I have discovered is that what turns customers *into loyal customers who return* is connection. When you have connection, you have something that binds you.

JUST A PINCH OF CREATIVITY CAN GO A LONG WAY.

For instance, Starbucks did something I thought was really creative. Employees glued or taped a fake cup of coffee on the roof of a car and drove around the city. It's pretty common when you are rushing out the door to forget your cup of Joe on top of the car. So, as they drove around, people would kindly yell out, *"Your coffee is on your roof!"* For every person who said something, they handed out a coupon to free coffee at Starbucks. This creative idea got media coverage and probably made a lot of people's days brighter. Was it good for business? You bet!

If you don't have a lot of money and want to do something special for someone, just take a moment to think creatively. Invite others into your thinking process. Their suggestions may stir up some good ideas. Not every creative idea will have wings to fly, but you just never know. Look at this book! Who would have thought.

I have some friends who were short on cash, but on date night, instead of staying in, they went to visit really nice hotels in the city of Chicago and drink coffee. Some of the hotels in Chicago are really nice places to just sit, relax and people watch. It's fun.

An act of creativity can make someone's day.

To grow in business or a relationship, you have to be open to feedback, suggestions and ideas. Take a moment to think what gifts, ideas or philosophies you possess that you could use to create a creative (a.k.a "lizard") experience? One of my friends sends out a minimum of two thank you cards each week. I asked him once, *"What if you have no one to thank?"* His response was, *"There is always someone to thank. Plus, people notice this and really appreciate it. It strengthens my connections with others."*

When I set up our company payroll with ADP, their rep got our company a pie with forks and a note saying, *"I am hungry for your business."* I loved that! (I ate the pie, and they got my business.) If you are hungry for my business, my address is at the end of this book. Feel free to send me food – make sure it's yummy.

*"Creativity requires
the courage to let go
of certainties."*

Erich Fromm

The Lizard....
Creates "Better Service" for YOU

"I'll get nicer when you get smarter."

Larry Winget

Ever had such bad service that you imagined saying to that person, *"I want to fire you and make sure you never work in this town again!"* I have. As I mentioned earlier, some people don't understand how the experiences they create for others directly effect their lives, success and relationships. Perhaps no one ever explained it to them.

There is NOT a lot of value in becoming a full-time complainer and criticizer. So a few years ago, I began to apply the lizard experience to get better service. I realized you cannot force others to care, but you *can* be an example for them to follow and learn from. If someone is having a bad day, it's easy to tell, because their attitude is letting you know about it and their service is expressing it. So the key for you is getting through all the junk to get to that person's best. After all, that's what we want, isn't it – their best service? Remember, this does not mean manipulating people to get what you want. It's doing two things: setting an example of what you want, and bringing out someone's best.

One couple applied this principle after hearing me speak on this topic. In my programs, I often say, *"If a Tic-tac can make a difference, then so can you."* My personal favorite is, *"If you want to make someone's day, go buy them a Happy Meal from McDonalds. Put it down in front of them, and when they ask what this is for, you just tell them, 'It's a Happy Meal. If you eat it, it will make you happy.'"*

Gets a smile every time.

I have purchased a lot of Happy Meals for others over the years. *(Sometimes I treat myself to a Happy Meal - a few of them. Hey, there's nothing wrong with getting happy... right?)*

Well, this couple was waiting in the checkout line and noticed that the gentleman at the register was being quite rude to the people ahead of them. When they stepped up, they were also treated rudely. The wife was so mad, she wanted to go find the manager and complain, which is a popular reaction to poor service. However, the husband said, *"Let's do something different. Let's go buy him a Happy Meal."* The wife was like, *" A HAPPY WHAT?!"*

But reluctantly agreed. They got back in line when they returned, and when they stepped up, they just put the Happy Meal down. The gentleman asked, *"What's this?"*

"It seems like you are having a tough day, so we thought a Happy Meal might cheer you up a little."

They said the guy about broke down in tears. He said it was one of the nicest things anyone had ever done. The couple then asked, *"Do you think next time we come back, you will treat us better?"*

The gentleman, somewhat embarrassed by his behavior said, *"I will treat you right."*

I also once applied this with a taxi cab driver. He was very cranky when he picked us up and even more cranky when he found out that we didn't have far to go. I told him not to worry, that I would make it worth his time. He didn't really get what I was saying. When he dropped us off, he didn't even help us with the luggage. When he got out to get paid, the fare was only seven bucks, but, I gave him $50 and said, *"I told you I would make it worth your time."* The expression on his face changed from cranky to grateful. He about melted. His face didn't look angry or tense. He looked grateful and excited. I then looked at him and boldly said, *"You be nice! If you do, it will pay off!"*

He shook his head in agreement and even though I didn't get his best service, I am sure I put something in motion for the next customer to get treated better.

You don't always need money to bring out someone's best. Just use the best of who you are. You can compliment someone – their shoes, hair, teeth, car, name, whatever. Be like Luke Skywalker in *Star Wars,* when he kept saying to Darth Vader (his real father), *"I know there is good in you, Father."*

Hey, if you have to say it to someone, say it. I have said this to many cranky people. *"I know there is good in you."*

You might get an odd look, but who cares? You are letting them know something that they may not know, and that's a good thing.

Ever ask for something and the response is an unenthusiastic, *"Let me see what I can do."*

In that case, I like to kindly say, *"I believe in you!"*

One woman was "so called" trying to help with something, and I got the vibe that she was not really connected to helping me. I had a pizza with me and I put it up on the counter and I said, *"If you can make this happen (what I wanted), there is a nice warm slice of pepperoni pizza in it for you."*

Her face perked up with a smile, and she said, *"Well in that case, let's make this happen for you!"*

Here is why this principle has better results than complaining.

Let's say you give the person the best of who you are and they still treat you rudely. It will happen. Sometimes, you won't be able to break down the walls of other people. For some unknown reason, life has hardened their souls. Would you agree?

It's evident that now more than ever, we live in reactive times. If someone cuts us off in traffic, our initial gut response might be to speed up and cut him or her off – give him a taste of his own doing. If someone yells at us or is rude to us, our brain may instantly say, *"Hey, I don't deserve this. And just to show you how much I disapprove of your treatment, here is a little dirt right back atcha!"*

That's how things get out of control. That's how stress builds up and emergency rooms get filled with heart attack victims and stab wounds. (*I am guessing on the stab wounds, but some people do some crazy things.*)

However, I use this principle with confidence that it will work more times in my favor than not. I have used this principle to my advantage on the phone, at local stores, with airlines, in traffic, and it's worked much more in my favor than flipping out. I'll be honest; there have been moments when I have felt more like flipping out. Somehow, some people just know how to bring your "flip" out. *(I think you know what I mean.)* But instead, make it a habit in those situations to do what you want others to see you do. Create the example for others to follow. In essence you are giving them a gift that will work in favor for them. If they happen to grasp the concept and apply it, eventually it will reward them. All thanks to you!

Use this principle to create great service from your vendors.

Ever worked with a big or small company and they didn't do what they said they would do? You felt like your job order or project got stuck on the back burner for something more profitable to them?

Another way of looking at it is you might think that if someone is selling you something or offers you a service, it's in their best interest to take care of you. As true as that might be, again I use this principle in a way that works in my favor, so I don't have to worry about being put on the backburner. I am too emotional to sit and wonder when it will be my turn, when I will get my order or project complete. What I like to do for those who are my vendors (those who offer me products and services) is to create a good customer experience for them. I might send them a thank you card. At Christmas, I send them cookies. I will send birthday cards. We do a lot of fun things for our vendors. We let them know how much we appreciate their attention to detail and their response time. And we really do!

The results of applying this principle is we get great service. Speedy service. Quality service. Personal attention. We may not be the biggest client they have, but they know one thing about working with us: we create a great experience for them. They are going to experience recognition and appreciation from us. They are going to feel how important and valuable they are. Now, let me ask you this: if you got that on a regular basis, would you give it personal attention? Sure you would.

*"Those who bring
sunshine into the lives
of others, cannot keep
it from themselves."*

James M. Barrie

The Lizard....
Creates Inspirational Leadership

"Those who accept the responsibility of leadership roles, must embrace the value and best practices of bringing out the best in others."

Sam Glenn

"You don't need a title to be a leader."

Mark Sanborn

Years ago, I was invited to speak at a celebration banquet. I sat at my table, drinking coffee and prepping my notes for the group. People started filling the room, and the vibe I got was that it was a very depressed work environment. As I looked around, I really felt badly for this group. There was such a lack of energy and enthusiasm. I even asked the meeting planner, *"Is everything okay? Did someone die?"*

She said, *"Nope, that's just how it is here. There have been a lot of changes. People have become negative. Our turnover rate is pretty high. I think people come to work scared. They don't know what to expect; so they work in fear."*

When the CEO who was to speak before me arrived, I began to put the puzzle together. I have learned over the years that you can hold a title, but it doesn't mean you possess good leadership.

I noticed the CEO was stand-offish. He didn't approach anyone, shake hands, crack a smile or anything. He had that "all about business look," but it was supposed to be a celebration banquet. Something didn't add up. I knew he was the CEO and had a lot on his plate, but he owned more than the title. He owned the responsibility to lead and inspire his company to greatness, no matter the circumstances.

When the event started, they showed a 30-minute video about the history of the company which was comparable to a good sleeping pill. When they woke me up (heh), the CEO got up to talk. If it was a football pep talk, we would have gotten beat by 100 points. Instead of recognizing, rewarding, affirming and inspiring, all he did was talk numbers. In fact, he talked about the market and how shaky it was and that we should hope for the best. *(Well, if that little speech doesn't keep you up at night, just plop in the video again.)*

He was instilling fear into his work force. Was he the corporate boogey man? Because he sure wasn't inspiring or reassuring. I wanted to offer him this insight, *"The market may stink, but you don't have to. You can choose to be better than the situation. History has proven, there is always a way."*

He treated his work force like strangers. In reality, he saw his work force as robots. No wonder this group lacked passion, connection and team spirit. If he wanted to get their best, he needed to use some inspiration. Inspiration unlocks potential, gives us hope, and opens the mind to be more creative. Inspiration is not the only element that rallies the troops, but it is a necessity. When I played college basketball, my coach never got up and said, "Okay, guys, I just saw the other team. They are huge and chances are they could beat you up pretty bad. Good luck out there and let's hope for the best."

We never would have won if we heard something like that. Teams that win do so because they are fed the vitamins of inspiration. If you skip taking your vitamins, chances are you can get sick, become unhealthy and ineffective.

This style of leadership is highly destructive to growth and success. Here is the result of treating your employees, staff or team like robots:

When you do, it will eventually cost you more. You aren't maximizing a person's potential. Instead, your business will be like the one in the movie, *Office Space*. It's about unmotivated, under-appreciated employees who do *just enough* so they won't get fired. Think about it; let's say you are a parent and you hired someone to watch your kids for seven hours. Would you be okay if you paid them for the full seven hours, but they only watched them for about five of those hours? That's the way it has become for so many. They are not connected to what they do, therefore there is a lack of passion and desire to press on towards the vision. So, how does one change all of that?

> *The deepest craving of human nature*
> *is the need to be appreciated.*
>
> *William James*

In Mathew Kelly's book, <u>The Dream Manager</u>, he talks about helping others become the best version of themselves, and that the result will be the company inevitably becoming the best version of itself. What that entails is focusing on more than just raises and bonuses (although those do help).

You must pay attention to the needs of others. If you are a Zig Ziglar fan, you have heard him for years say, *"If you help enough people get what they want, you will get what you want."*

The lizard experience involves finding ways to recognize and reward those who make the company run. Employees are the first group of customers a company interacts with. If they aren't valued, they will not value others. It will be a "just getting by" sort of relationship. *"Give me what I want, and I will give you some of what you want."* Are you getting the picture?

I remember doing an internship for one of the largest consulting firms in the world. At the time, they were number one in their market. One of the things I did to keep myself inspired was to put positive quotes on the white board. One day, a VP in upper-ultra-management from the heavens above stopped down to say hi. He gave me some personal attention, talked to me about my goals, and in the end thanked me for being an asset to the company and taking initiative to keep others positive.

Did that mean something to me? You bet. It was fuel for the fire. I felt valued and important. And because of that, I actually wanted to give my best. My desire to be loyal and work hard for the company grew.

The lizard experience applied to leadership means taking the fear out of work. It's inspiring others and finding ways to bring out their best by paying attention to their needs and treating them like valuable assets, not just weekly expenses. The benefit to you is that the company's bottom line will increase, turnover will decrease, and your initial group of customers will become more effective, as connected and passionate employees.

"We make a living by what we get, but we make a life by what we give."

Winston Churchill

The Lizard...
Creates a Lasting and
Worthwhile Legacy

When you look back on your time,
what will you see - footprints
in the sand or butt prints?

Be to someone what someone was to
you. You might only be one person in
a large world, but to that one person,
you just might be the whole world.

I was looking out the window, waiting for my flight to board (if you notice, I tell a lot of travel stories; that's because I travel a lot). As I was waiting in the crowded airport, I noticed an elderly woman trying to call her family to let them know about what time she and her husband might be arriving. This was before cell phones were highly accessible. She didn't have enough change, so I politely pulled out a calling card and offered it to her. She gratefully took the card and used it to call her family.

A gentleman sitting next to me leaned over and

said, *"I am glad there are people like you. I couldn't help thinking if that was my mom or grandma, how I would want them to be treated in a situation like that. What you did was really nice."*

The elderly woman walked back over to give me the calling card back and I said, *"I have another one; you go ahead and keep that one."*

At first she was resistant. Then I overheard her talking to her husband saying, *"Look, Honey, that nice young man just gave me his credit card!"*

To which the guy next to me said, *"Wow, you are generous!"*

I laughed and walked over to explain that it wasn't a credit card, that it was a calling card.

The "lizard experience" has gone on for more than a decade, and now I am extending the benefits of the experience to others by telling the story and giving away small plastic lizards at my speaking engagements. My mom started something that she will always be known for – hiding the lizard in my lasagna. Her one simple action created a legacy. We all have that ability. Creating a legacy involves caring enough to put others first and give them your best – that in essence is what the whole lizard experience is. The by-product is getting what you desire.

Put your "spectacular" into action and you will create your legacy.

What do you want to be remembered for? I, personally, want to be known for my kindness and sincerity. I believe that's part of my "extra-special" signature. I like to do nice things for others. I guess the reason why this is so meaningful for me is because of all of those who have done kind things for me. It's moved me to do the same. Plus, it's a pet peeve to see rudeness in action. There is not a single benefit to being rude. NONE.

I remember being so sleepy on a flight home, that I fell asleep on the shoulder of the woman next to me. When I woke up, I started laughing and apologized. She smiled and said, *"It was my pleasure. You are welcome to finish your nap there if you like."* It was a sweet and sincere gesture.

To act with kindness is an opportunity to build into my legacy. If you act on what's meaningful to you, it will build into your legacy. Maybe it's getting involved with a cause that helps children with cancer. Maybe it's being a source of encouragement for others. We've all had moments when we we've been down, and wondered who we could call on to lift us up. *Your legacy builds when you choose to be that person for someone else!*

What do you want to be remembered for?

What stands out about you that says you made a footprint in the sands of time?

*Be to somebody else
what somebody has
been to you.*

*"Life is an opportunity
for you to contribute
love in your own way."*

Bernie Siegal, M.D.

Let's wrap it up and call it a day!

The "lizard" experience has taught me some pretty simple, yet life-enriching lessons. Looking back, I am just thankful that Mom didn't put a fake spider or snake in the lasagna. I'm not sure I could have handled that, but overall I have come to appreciate and draw upon the dynamic of this lesson. One point to remember before we close up shop here is that you don't need a plastic lizard to achieve more of what you desire in life. The "essence" of the lizard is already with you. You showed up on this planet with amazing gifts and abilities; if you apply them right where you are now, you will begin to experience more of what you want. It's that simple. Plus, as an added bonus, when you develop the right relationships with those who do the same, bigger things will happen!

The one trait that can keep us from moving forward or using the gifts we have is this thing called "doubt." It is the killer of dreams, relationships and new opportunities. When you doubt yourself, you defeat yourself. Doubt tries to keep us from our best. It has us questioning our efforts and the greatness that we were born with. It attacks us when we fail-- through negative people or by showing up unexpectedly in our thoughts. Doubt does not work for you, so don't employ it.

Belief in yourself does work. You have everything to gain when believing in "YOU" in a healthy and positive way. You don't have to be perfect, or compare yourself to others, but you can choose to be amazing with the greatness you were born with. And in doing so, you will discover that what you want and what wants you will progress towards one another.

I personally look for opportunities every day to apply this lesson, which is to use the best of who I am to create the best of what I want. Again, it's not about acquiring stuff. Some of us have so much stuff, we need to have a garage sale! Instead, this is about gaining what is meaningful and making your life worthwhile. My hope is that you will embrace these ideas and make them your own, as they will only work for you if you take them home with you.

Meet the Author, Sam Glenn,
The Authority On Attitude!™

Sam Glenn currently resides in Chicago, Illinois. He lives minutes from where they film Oprah, and dreams about the day he will be a guest on the show and jump on all the furniture like Tom Cruise did (well, okay, maybe not quite like that). Sam has become one of the most in-demand, premier inspirational and motivational keynote speakers in the country. This once night-time janitor who slept on borrowed floor space now invigorates audiences of every size and some as large as 75,000, with side-splitting humor, inspirational insights and candid simplicity.

Tell someone about this book!
Send them to our website: Samglenn.com.
While you're there, sign up for our
incredible newsletter - Attitude Kickers!

Information on Booking Sam to Speak to Your Group:
Visit:Samglenn.com
Email: contact@samglenn.com
800-818-6378

Check out Sam Glenn's Incredible DVD Series,
"A Kick in the Attitude".
It's the perfect way to keep your team motivated!
Visit EverythingAttitude.com

LizardBook.com

Michelle Arnold – Thank you for always being there, being supportive and building this company to what it is.

Susan and Andy Warcaba – Without your nuttiness and leftovers, there would be no Lizard story to tell. Thank you for your love and support.

Steve and Kathy Dawidiuk – Thank you for years of support. You guys have been there since day one and are always there for me. You truly define friendship.

Chris & Melissa Glenn – Thank you for all ways being there for me. I am grateful for all your encouragement and understanding from day one.

Ben & Polina Glenn - Thank you for all the dysfunction you bring to my life. Your help in my work has touched so many people. Thank you.

Jocelyn Godfrey – thank you for helping me make sense of words.

Kirsten and Loretta at RE: Invention – Thanks for making sense of my nonsense.

RJ Communications - Thanks for the paper & great service!

Phil Studdard – Flip Design – "YOU ROCK! There may not be a better graphic designer on the planet."

Frank Shelton – thank you for your humor and support.

Randy Hosilyk – thank you for being patient with all of our book changes.

There are so many more I want to thank – friends and family and I just want you to know how grateful I am for you.

Dan Ondra - Thank you for making me look so good on the web! Your wisdom is priceless and your encouragement a stepping stone.